973 Kal

alman, B.
potlight on the United
tates of America.

FEB 2 8 20██

3593/tl   )

GEORGINA PUBLIC LIBRARIES
PETER GZOWSKI BRANCH
5279 BLACK RIVER ROAD
P.O. BX 338, SUTTON, ON LOE 1R0

Spotlight on the
United States
of America

Bobbie Kalman and Niki Walker

🌴 Crabtree Publishing Company

www.crabtreebooks.com

Created by Bobbie Kalman

For Niki, Josh, and Jack, with love from Bobbie

Editor-in-Chief
Bobbie Kalman

Writing team
Bobbie Kalman
Niki Walker

Editor
Robin Johnson

Photo research
Crystal Sikkens

Design
Bobbie Kalman
Katherine Kantor
Robert MacGregor
  (front cover)

Production coordinator
Katherine Kantor

Illustrations
Barbara Bedell: pages 14-15 (bottom), 23 (middle)
Katherine Kantor: pages 4, 5, 6-7, 8
Bonna Rouse: back cover (eagle), pages 12, 14 (top), 15 (top), 23 (bottom),
  28 (top left)
Margaret Amy Salter: page 24 (top)

Photographs
© Crabtree Publishing Company: page 16
The Granger Collection, New York: pages 22 (right), 24 (bottom)
© iStockphoto.com: pages 12 (top left), 26 (top), 29 (right), 31 (mask)
© 2008 Jupiterimages Corporation: pages 6 (left), 13 (bottom), 17 (top)
Library of Congress. World Telegram & Sun photo by Dick DeMarsico:
  page 27 (top)
© ShutterStock.com: back cover, pages 1, 3, 5, 6 (right), 8, 9, 10, 11, 12
  (bottom right), 13 (all except bottom), 17 (bottom), 18, 19, 21, 22 (left),
  25, 27 (bottom), 28 (bottom right), 29 (left), 30, 31 (top, middle right,
  and bottom left)
Other images by Digital Stock, Digital Vision, and Image Club Graphics

Library and Archives Canada Cataloguing in Publication

Kalman, Bobbie, 1947-
    Spotlight on the United States of America / Bobbie Kalman and
Niki Walker.

(Spotlight on my country)
Includes index.
ISBN 978-0-7787-3452-9 (bound).--ISBN 978-0-7787-3478-9 (pbk.)

    1. United States--Juvenile literature. I. Walker, Niki, 1972- II. Title.
III. Series.

E156.K33 2007   j973   C2007-906309-8

Library of Congress Cataloging-in-Publication Data

Kalman, Bobbie.
  Spotlight on the United States of America / Bobbie Kalman and
Niki Walker.
       p. cm. -- (Spotlight on my country)
  Includes index.
  ISBN-13: 978-0-7787-3452-9 (rlb)
  ISBN-10: 0-7787-3452-8 (rlb)
  ISBN-13: 978-0-7787-3478-9 (pb)
  ISBN-10: 0-7787-3478-1 (pb)
    1. United States--Juvenile literature. I. Walker, Niki, 1972- II. Title.
III. Series.

E156.K337 2007
973--dc22
                                                    2007042629

Crabtree Publishing Company

www.crabtreebooks.com   1-800-387-7650

Copyright © **2008 CRABTREE PUBLISHING COMPANY**. All rights reserved. No part of this publication may be reproduced, stored in a retrieval system or be transmitted in any form or by any means, electronic, mechanical, photocopying, recording, or otherwise, without the prior written permission of Crabtree Publishing Company. In Canada: We acknowledge the financial support of the Government of Canada through the Book Publishing Industry Development Program (BPIDP) for our publishing activities.

Published in Canada
Crabtree Publishing
616 Welland Ave.
St. Catharines, Ontario
L2M 5V6

Published in the United States
Crabtree Publishing
PMB16A
350 Fifth Ave., Suite 3308
New York, NY 10118

Published in the United Kingdom
Crabtree Publishing
White Cross Mills
High Town, Lancaster
LA1 4XS

Published in Australia
Crabtree Publishing
386 Mt. Alexander Rd.
Ascot Vale (Melbourne)
VIC 3032

Contents

The United States

Welcome to the United States of America! The United States of America is also known as the United States, America, or the U.S.A. The United States is a **country**. A country is an area of land that has people. It has **laws**, or rules, that people must follow. A country also has **borders** that separate it from neighboring countries. The United States has two neighbors. Canada is its neighbor to the north. Mexico is its neighbor to the south.

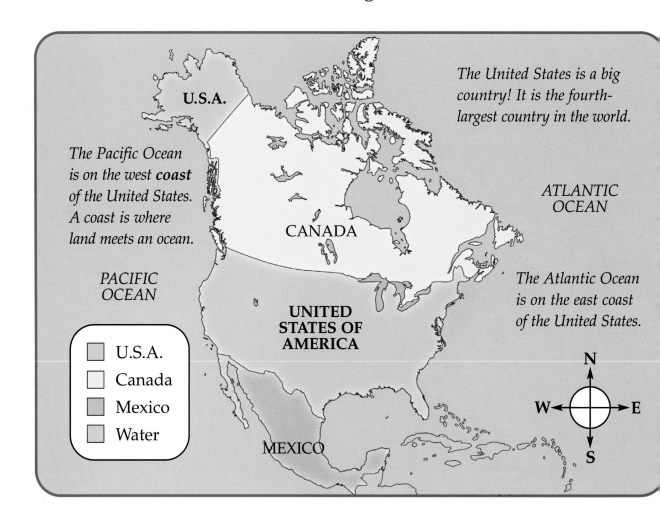

U.S.A.

The United States is a big country! It is the fourth-largest country in the world.

The Pacific Ocean is on the west coast of the United States. A coast is where land meets an ocean.

CANADA

ATLANTIC OCEAN

PACIFIC OCEAN

The Atlantic Ocean is on the east coast of the United States.

UNITED STATES OF AMERICA

- ☐ U.S.A.
- ☐ Canada
- ☐ Mexico
- ☐ Water

MEXICO

N W E S

Where is the United States?

The United States is part of the **continent** of North America. A continent is a huge area of land. There are seven continents on Earth. They are North America, South America, Europe, Asia, Africa, Australia and Oceania, and Antarctica. Find all the continents on the map below.

Which two continents can you see on the globe that the girl above is holding?

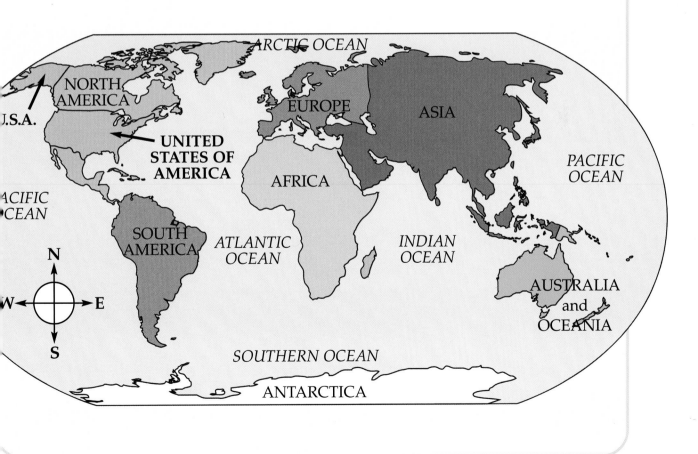

5

Fifty states

The United States is made up of fifty **states**. Forty-eight of the states are located between Canada and Mexico. Two states, Alaska and Hawaii, do not touch the other states. Alaska is in the Far North. Canada separates it from the rest of the U.S.A. Hawaii is a group of **islands** in the Pacific Ocean. Islands are pieces of land that have water all around them.

PACIFIC OCEAN

Alaska is a very cold place. The land is covered with snow and ice. Arctic foxes live there.

*In Hawaii, the weather is warm all year. There are huge ocean waves. It is a great place for **surfing**! Surfing is riding waves on a special board.*

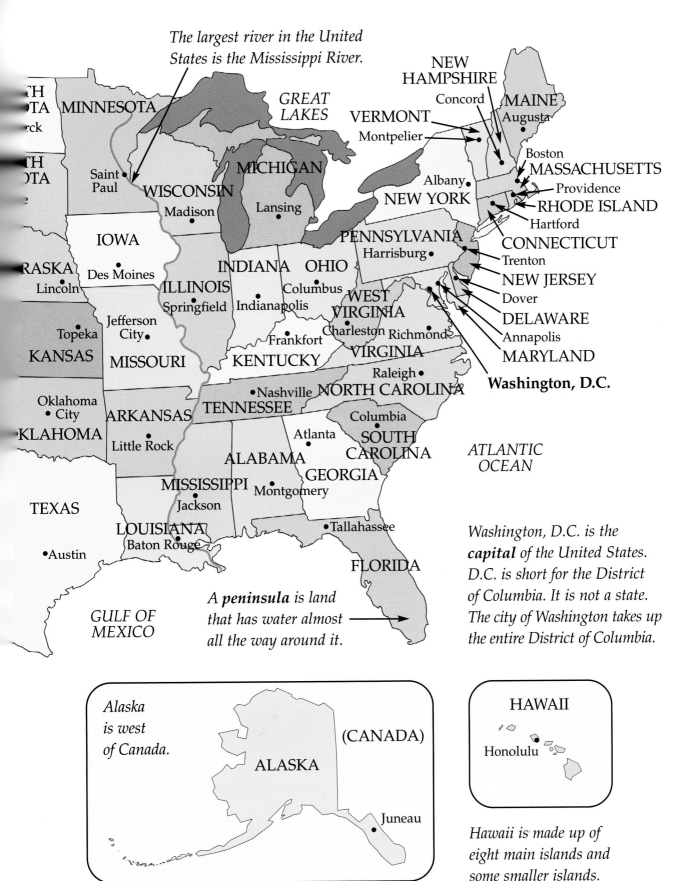

The largest river in the United States is the Mississippi River.

GREAT LAKES

NEW HAMPSHIRE

Concord

MAINE

Augusta

VERMONT

Montpelier

MINNESOTA

Saint Paul

MICHIGAN

Lansing

WISCONSIN

Madison

IOWA

Des Moines

Boston

MASSACHUSETTS

Providence

RHODE ISLAND

Hartford

CONNECTICUT

Albany

NEW YORK

PENNSYLVANIA

Harrisburg

Trenton

NEW JERSEY

Dover

DELAWARE

Annapolis

MARYLAND

Washington, D.C.

INDIANA OHIO

Columbus

ILLINOIS

Springfield Indianapolis

WEST VIRGINIA

Charleston Richmond

VIRGINIA

RASKA

Lincoln

Jefferson City

Topeka

KANSAS

MISSOURI

Frankfort

KENTUCKY

Raleigh

Nashville NORTH CAROLINA

Oklahoma City

ARKANSAS

TENNESSEE

Columbia

Atlanta

SOUTH CAROLINA

ATLANTIC OCEAN

OKLAHOMA

Little Rock

ALABAMA

GEORGIA

MISSISSIPPI Montgomery

TEXAS

Jackson

LOUISIANA

Baton Rouge

Austin

Tallahassee

FLORIDA

A **peninsula** is land that has water almost all the way around it.

GULF OF MEXICO

Washington, D.C. is the **capital** of the United States. D.C. is short for the District of Columbia. It is not a state. The city of Washington takes up the entire District of Columbia.

Alaska is west of Canada.

(CANADA)

ALASKA

Juneau

HAWAII

Honolulu

Hawaii is made up of eight main islands and some smaller islands.

7

America's land

The desert above has mountains behind it. This landscape is in the Southwest area of the United States. The climate in this area is hot and dry.

The United States has many **landscapes**. A landscape is how land looks. Landscapes include forests, mountains, **deserts**, beaches, and **plains**. Plains are flat, grassy areas. The United States also has different **climates**. Climate is the usual weather in an area.

Five regions

The United States can be divided into five **regions**, or areas. The five regions are shown on this map. They are the Northwest, the Southwest, the Midwest, the Northeast, and the Southeast. Each region is made up of several states. The states in a region have similar landscapes and climates.

NORTHWEST

SOUTHWEST

MIDWEST

NORTHEAST

SOUTHEAST

The Northwest is warm during most of the year. This region gets a lot of rain. Thick forests with huge trees grow there.

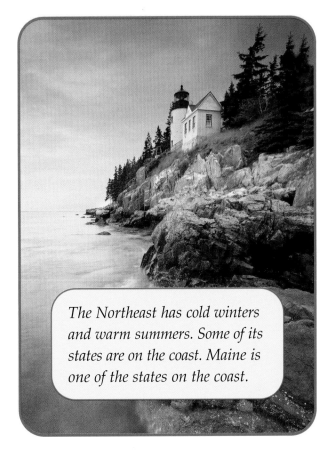

The Northeast has cold winters and warm summers. Some of its states are on the coast. Maine is one of the states on the coast.

The Midwest also has cold winters and warm summers. Parts of this region are flat and dry. Grasses, wheat, and corn grow well there.

The Southeast is warm or hot all year. It gets a lot of rain. There are often **hurricanes** in this region. Hurricanes are dangerous wind storms.

Plants and animals

Many kinds of plants grow in the United States. Many kinds of animals live there, too. The plants and animals are suited to their **habitats**, or the natural places where they grow or live. Some plants and animals are found only in one region. Others are found throughout the United States.

Iguanas live in deserts in the Southwest. They eat cactuses that grow in the deserts.

*Alligators live in **swamps** in the Southeast. Swamps are flat, wet areas with many plants.*

10

Conifer forests grow in many northern areas of the United States. Conifers are trees with cones. Their leaves are like needles. Moose eat conifer leaves. Very few other animals can eat these sharp leaves.

Cougars, which are also called mountain lions, live in many habitats in the United States. They can live high up on mountains or in northern forests. Some cougars even live in hot **rain forests**.

Who are Americans?

People who live in the United States are called Americans. Some American families have lived in the U.S.A. for hundreds of years. Other Americans have come to the country from different areas of the world. They brought parts of their **cultures**, or ways of life, to the United States.

Millions of people

The **population** of the United States is very large. Population is the number of people who live in a country. More than 301 million people live in the U.S.A.

American culture is popular all over the world.

The faces of America

People with many backgrounds live in the United States. These children may look different, but they are all Americans!

Most Americans speak English, but many also speak Spanish.

13

Native Americans

tipi

Native Americans were the first peoples to live in the United States. Hundreds of **nations**, or groups, lived across North America for thousands of years. Each nation had its own language, leaders, and way of life. Some nations lived in the Northeast, where they grew corn and other foods. Some lived on the plains, where they hunted buffalo for their meat and **hides**, or skins.

*(left) People who hunted buffalo lived in homes called **tipis**. Tipis were made from buffalo hides.*

Several native nations lived around the Great Lakes.

pueblo

People who lived in the Southwest built huge homes called **pueblos**. Pueblos were made of clay and mud.

The colonies

Hundreds of years ago, the United States was not a country. Only native people lived there. In the 1500s and 1600s, other countries took over parts of North America. England, France, and Spain set up **colonies** there. A colony is a place that is ruled by a faraway country. People who lived in the colonies were called **colonists**.

*English colonists first **settled**, or lived, where the state of Virginia is today. The colonists traveled by ship across the Atlantic Ocean. They built a fort, called James Fort, on the coast.*

The Thirteen Colonies

By the 1700s, England had thirteen colonies along the Atlantic Ocean. The King of England controlled the colonies. The colonists had to obey the laws that the king made. They also had to pay **taxes** to the king on any money they made.

Some colonists were very wealthy.

*The **governor** acted on behalf of the King of England. He lived in a beautiful palace in Williamsburg, Virginia.*

Fighting for freedom

By the late 1700s, many people in the colonies wanted **independence**. Independence is the freedom to rule one's own country. The colonists had to fight England for independence. Their fight was called the **American Revolution**. A revolution is a war against the rulers of a country. The **American Revolutionary War** began in 1775.

Thomas Jefferson

Benjamin Franklin

John Adams

I do declare!

The **Declaration of Independence** was written during the American Revolution. This **document** stated that the colonists wanted to make their own laws in their own country. It also listed complaints about England and the king. Leaders of the colonies signed it on July 4, 1776.

Thomas Jefferson wrote the Declaration of Independence. This picture shows him with two of the men who signed it.

The Americans won the revolution in 1781. The Thirteen Colonies became the United States of America. In 1789, George Washington became the first American **president**.

George Washington

Georgina Public Libraries, Peter Gzowski Branch

The government

*The President lives and works in the White House in Washington, D.C. The **Vice President** also works there.*

Americans had to decide how to rule their country. They did not want one ruler to have all the power, the way the King of England had. They made a set of rules for the **government** to follow. A government is in charge of a country or part of a country. The set of rules that the government follows is called the **Constitution**.

A democracy

The United States is a **federal republic**. The government of a federal republic is a **democracy**. In a democracy, people **elect**, or choose, their leaders. Americans elect a president every four years. The President is the head of the government. The government makes laws in the United States Capitol, shown right.

*The U.S. Supreme Court is made up of nine **justices**, or judges. The justices make sure that the laws are fair and that people follow them.*

*Americans **vote** to elect their president.*

21

Moving west

When the United States became a country, it was much smaller than it is today. Then, in 1803, President Thomas Jefferson bought a huge piece of land from France. The purchase was called the **Louisiana Purchase**. The United States also got land in the West from Mexico. President Jefferson sent two men to explore the land. Meriwether Lewis and William Clark traveled all the way to the Pacific Ocean. They made maps and wrote notes about the West.

A Native American woman named Sacagawea helped the explorers make the trip safely.

In the 1800s, many Americans moved west. They wanted to build homes on their own land. At first, the **pioneers** made the long trip across the country in wagons. A long line of wagons traveling together was called a **wagon train**.

a wagon train

More and more people moved west. They built farms, ranches, and **boomtowns**. Boomtowns were towns that grew quickly. Then, the railway was built across America, and many more people settled in the West.

a ranch

a boomtown

The end of slavery

In the 1600s, colonists sent ships to Africa to bring back **slaves**. Slaves are people who are owned by other people. They are forced to work very hard without being paid. For hundreds of years, African Americans were slaves in the South. Some people helped slaves run away to northern states or to Canada, where they could be free. This group of people was known as the **Underground Railroad**.

People in the Underground Railroad hid slaves in wagons and houses. They helped the slaves travel north to safety.

This picture shows what a battle was like during the Civil War.

The Civil War

People in the North wanted to **abolish**, or put an end to, slavery in the United States. They went to war to stop slavery. The war was called the **Civil War**. It was a war between two groups of Americans. Soldiers from the northern states were in the **Union Army**. They fought the **Confederate Army** of the southern states. In 1865, the North won the war. President Abraham Lincoln ordered the **emancipation** of slaves in America. Emancipation means setting free.

The Confederate Army carried this flag.

This is a statue of Abraham Lincoln with the American flag.

American holidays

Americans celebrate many holidays. Some holidays are **national holidays**. National holidays honor important events or people in a country's past. These pages show some national holidays that are celebrated in the United States.

The **Fourth of July** is the biggest national holiday. It is also called **Independence Day**. Independence Day celebrates the day the Declaration of Independence was signed. Americans think of this day as their country's "birthday." They celebrate with parades, parties, and fireworks.

Martin Luther King Day is celebrated on the third Monday in January. Martin Luther King Jr., shown right, worked hard in the 1960s to gain **equality** for African Americans. Equality means being treated the same as others.

Memorial Day is on the last Monday in May. On this day, Americans remember the people who fought and died for their country.

Thanksgiving is celebrated on the fourth Thursday of November. On Thanksgiving Day, Americans think about the things for which they are grateful. Most people celebrate by having turkey dinners with their families.

American symbols

These pages show some American **symbols**. A symbol is a sign or picture that **represents**, or stands for, something else. Some symbols stand for countries, power, or freedom. Find out what each of these American symbols represents.

The bald eagle

The bald eagle is the symbol of America. It is a large, strong bird that soars high and flies freely. Bald eagles are found only in North America.

America's flag

The American flag is known as the **Stars and Stripes**, the **Star Spangled Banner**, and **Old Glory**. Its thirteen red and white stripes represent the Thirteen Colonies. The flag has fifty stars, one for each of America's states.

Lady Liberty

The **Statue of Liberty** is a symbol of freedom. In one hand, Lady Liberty holds a torch that stands for **liberty**. In her other hand, she holds a tablet with "July 4, 1776" written on it. The Statue of Liberty was a gift to the United States from France.

The Liberty Bell

The **Liberty Bell** is another symbol of freedom to Americans. This large bell rang when the Declaration of Independence was first read in public. It was read on July 8, 1776, in Philadelphia, Pennsylvania.

Guess the city!

The United States is known for its beautiful and interesting cities. How much do you know about them? For example, do you know which city has the most crooked street in the world? Take this quiz and see how much you know about America's cities.

1. (above) Lombard Street is the name of the most crooked street. In which American city is it located?

2. (left) Which city has huge waterfalls? Hint: Canada shares these waterfalls with the United States.

3. Which city is part of the United States but is far out in the ocean? Hint: It has beautiful beaches and warm weather all year.

4. Which city has this sign? Hint: This city is famous for movies and movie stars!

6. Which city is known for its tall buildings and many theaters?

5. Which city is known for its music, parades, and celebrations called Mardi Gras? Hint: This city was badly damaged by Hurricane Katrina in 2005.

a Mardi Gras mask

Answers:

1. San Francisco, California
2. Niagara Falls, New York
3. Honolulu, Hawaii
4. Los Angeles, California
5. New Orleans, Louisiana
6. New York, New York

Glossary

Note: Some boldfaced words are defined where they appear in the book.

capital The city in which the government of a country or state is located

colony An area that belongs to a country that is far away and which is ruled by that country

democracy A system of government that is run by elected leaders

desert A hot area that receives very little rain

document A piece of paper that contains important information

elect To choose a leader by voting

governor The person who represented the king in the Thirteen Colonies

liberty The freedom to act, speak, and think the way one chooses

pioneer A person who lives in a place before many other people live there

president The leader of a country

rain forest A thick forest that receives a lot of rain

state A part of a country that has its own people, leaders, and rules

tax Money paid to a government

vice president The person who ranks second to a president and takes the place of the president when necessary

vote To choose one person from a list of people

Index

Printed in the U.S.A.